T0402799

Get Motoring!

Boats

by Dalton Rains

FOCUS READERS®

SCOUT

www.focusreaders.com

Focus Readers is distributed by North Star Editions:
sales@northstareditions.com | 888-417-0195

Produced for Focus Readers by Red Line Editorial.

Photographs ©: Shutterstock Images, cover, 1, 4, 7 (top), 7 (bottom), 9 (top), 9 (bottom), 11, 13 (top), 13 (bottom), 15, 16 (top left), 16 (bottom left), 16 (bottom right); iStockphoto, 16 (top right)

Library of Congress Cataloging-in-Publication Data
Names: Rains, Dalton, author.
Title: Boats / by Dalton Rains.
Description: Mendota Heights, MN : Focus Readers, [2024] | Series: Get motoring! | Includes index. | Audience: Grades K-1
Identifiers: LCCN 2023029835 (print) | LCCN 2023029836 (ebook) | ISBN 9798889980063 (hardcover) | ISBN 9798889980490 (paperback) | ISBN 9798889981343 (pdf) | ISBN 9798889980926 (ebook)
Subjects: LCSH: Boats and boating--Juvenile literature.
Classification: LCC VM150 .R35 2024 (print) | LCC VM150 (ebook) | DDC 623.82--dc23/eng/20230727
LC record available at https://lccn.loc.gov/2023029835
LC ebook record available at https://lccn.loc.gov/2023029836

Printed in the United States of America
Mankato, MN
012024

About the Author

Dalton Rains is a writer and editor who lives in Minnesota.

Table of Contents

Boats

Boats float on the water.

They go on rivers, lakes,

and oceans.

A boat may stop

at a busy **harbor**.

Or a boat may stop

at a small dock.

harbor

dock

Parts

Most boats use **propellers**.

A propeller spins to make

the boat move.

Other boats use sails.

A sail catches the wind to make

the boat move.

propeller

sail

Uses

Many boats move **cargo**.

These boats are very large.

They go around the world.

cargo

Some boats carry people.

They can be small or large.

Some people ride them for fun.

Other boats are used for fishing.

Workers on the boats catch fish

for people to eat.

They use large **nets**.

net

Glossary

cargo

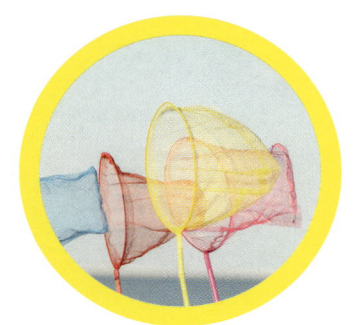

nets

harbor

propellers

Index